TYLER, THE CREATOR

BIOGRAPHY

The Life and Art of a Creative

Visionary

Jason T. Morgan

Copyright © 2025 by Jason T. Morgan

All rights reserved. No part of this publication may be reproduced, distributed, or transmitted in any form or by any means, including photocopying, recording, or other electronic or mechanical methods, without the prior written permission of the publisher, except in the case of brief quotations embodied in critical reviews and certain other noncommercial uses permitted by copyright law.

Table Of Contents

Introduction   7
   Purpose of the Biography   8

Chapter 1: Early Life and Background   11
   Childhood and Family Upbringing   11
   Musical Influences and Early Passions   12
   Growing Up in Los Angeles   14

Chapter 2: The Rise of Odd Future   17
   Formation of Odd Future   17
   Breakout Mixtape "Bastard" and Its Impact   18
   Odd Future's Cultural Movement   20

Chapter 3: Breakthrough with Goblin   23
   The Success of "Yonkers"   23
   Public Reception and Controversy   25
   Establishing His Identity in Hip-Hop   26

Chapter 4: Musical Evolution and Experimentation 29
   Albums: "Wolf", "Cherry Bomb", "Flower Boy", "Igor", and "Call Me If You Get Lost"   29
   Transition from Rap to Melodic and Experimental Styles   32
   Themes and Narratives in His Music   34

Chapter 5: Creative Ventures Beyond Music — 37
    Golf Wang Clothing Line and Merchandising — 37
    TV Show "Loiter Squad" and Acting Roles — 39
    Directing Music Videos and Visual Artistry — 40

Chapter 6: Awards and Recognition — 43
    Grammy Wins and Nominations — 43
    Cultural Impact and Influence on Modern Artists — 45
    Legacy as a Boundary-Breaking Artist — 46

Chapter 7: Personal Life and Philosophy — 49
    Views on Identity and Sexuality — 49
    Perspectives on Fame and Individuality — 50
    Relationships and Friendships in the Industry — 52

Chapter 8: Tyler's Influence on Culture and Fashion — 55
    Role in Redefining Masculinity in Hip-Hop — 55
    Contributions to Fashion and Style — 57
    Endorsements and Collaborations — 58
    Cultural Influence Beyond Fashion — 59

Chapter 9: Controversies and Public Image — 61
    Lyrics, Bans, and Public Reactions — 61
    Growth and Evolution Over the Years — 63
    Reframing His Public Image — 65

Chapter 10: The Future of Tyler, the Creator 67
    Potential Ventures in Film, Fashion, and Business 67
    His Lasting Impact on Art and Music 69

Conclusion 71

Introduction

Tyler, the Creator is a boundary-pushing artist whose innovative approach to music, fashion, and culture has earned him a reputation as one of the most creative and influential figures of his generation. Emerging from the underground with the controversial and raw energy of Odd Future Wolf Gang Kill Them All (OFWGKTA), Tyler shattered conventional expectations of what a hip-hop artist could be. His ability to blend genres, challenge norms, and remain unapologetically authentic has made him a trailblazer not only in music but in the broader cultural landscape.

From his debut mixtape "Bastard" to critically acclaimed albums like "Igor" and "Call Me If You Get Lost", Tyler has continuously evolved his sound, exploring themes of love, heartbreak, identity, and self-discovery. His artistry transcends traditional boundaries, often incorporating jazz, R&B, funk, and neo-soul into his productions. This genre-bending approach reflects his refusal to be boxed into any one category, a quality that has inspired a new wave of artists to embrace their individuality.

Beyond music, Tyler's ventures into fashion with his Golf Wang brand, his directorial work on music videos, and his creation of "Loiter Squad", a sketch comedy show, further underscore his multifaceted genius. His daring sense of style has redefined masculinity in hip-hop, challenging stereotypes and empowering others to express themselves freely. Tyler's fearless exploration of themes like sexuality and identity has also opened doors for broader conversations about inclusivity within the hip-hop community.

Purpose of the Biography

The purpose of this biography is to explore the life, artistry, and cultural significance of Tyler, the Creator in depth. While many know him as an eccentric and outspoken figure, few understand the journey that shaped him into the artist he is today. By examining his early life, career milestones, creative endeavors, and personal growth, this biography seeks to present a holistic view of Tyler's evolution from a rebellious teenager to a Grammy-winning artist and cultural icon.

This book aims to celebrate Tyler's contributions to music, fashion, and art while also digging into the challenges and controversies that have shaped his career. By highlighting his ability to turn adversity into innovation, readers will gain insight into the resilience and vision that define him. The biography also seeks to contextualize Tyler's influence on contemporary culture, showcasing how his fearlessness and authenticity have paved the way for a new generation of creators.

Ultimately, this biography is not just about Tyler's achievements but about his impact as a revolutionary force in a world that often resists change. His story serves as an inspiration for anyone striving to stay true to themselves while breaking barriers. As readers journey through Tyler's life, they will come to understand why he is not merely an artist but a cultural phenomenon whose legacy will continue to shape the future of music and art.

Chapter 1: Early Life and Background

Childhood and Family Upbringing

Tyler, The Creator, whose real name is Tyler Gregory Okonma, was born on March 6, 1991, in Hawthorne, California. He has a diverse background, with a Nigerian father of Igbo descent and an American mother with African-American and European-Canadian roots. Despite this heritage, he had no relationship with his father, who was absent during his upbringing. As a result, his mother took on the role of the main caregiver, working hard to support Tyler and his sister in Ladera Heights, a largely African-American area in Los Angeles County.

Growing up in a single-parent household, Tyler's mother instilled in him a strong sense of independence and creativity. He often credits her for supporting his dreams and providing the foundation for his success. Tyler also shared a close bond with his grandmother, who played an instrumental role in his upbringing. The absence of his father, though challenging, became a recurring theme in his music, where he often explored themes of identity, abandonment, and self-reliance.

Musical Influences and Early Passions

Even as a child, Tyler showed signs of his innate creativity. He would design imaginary album covers and create tracklists for non-existent records, showcasing a fascination with music production long before he ever touched an instrument. This early spark of imagination was a precursor to the unique artistry he would later bring to the music world.

At the age of 12, Tyler began experimenting with music production, using software like Reason and Fruity Loops to create beats. His early attempts were rudimentary, but they demonstrated his enthusiasm and willingness to learn. Recognizing her son's passion, his mother bought him a keyboard when he was 14. Tyler took it upon himself to teach himself how to play the piano, a skill that not only enhanced his musical understanding but also became a defining element of his sound.

Tyler's musical influences were as eclectic as his personality. He idolized Pharrell Williams and N.E.R.D., whose genre-blurring approach to music left a significant impact on him. He also drew inspiration from jazz, punk rock, and soul, absorbing a wide range of styles that would later shape his own genre-defying sound. Tyler's admiration for Pharrell's creativity and boldness would manifest in his own career as he consistently challenged industry norms and defied expectations.

Beyond music, Tyler was also passionate about skateboarding, graphic design, and filmmaking. These interests gave him a multidisciplinary perspective, allowing him to view creativity as an interconnected web rather than isolated disciplines. His diverse passions helped him build a multifaceted artistic identity that went beyond just being a rapper or producer.

Growing Up in Los Angeles

Los Angeles played a pivotal role in shaping Tyler's worldview and artistry. Growing up in Ladera Heights, often referred to as the "Black Beverly Hills," Tyler was exposed to a mix of privilege and struggle. While his neighborhood offered a sense of community and culture, the broader environment of Los Angeles exposed him to both the vibrancy and challenges of urban life.

The city's dynamic music scene became an integral part of Tyler's upbringing. From local underground rap battles to the mainstream success of West Coast hip-hop, Los Angeles offered a diverse blend of musical influences. Tyler absorbed this culture, blending it with his own unique ideas to create something entirely original.

However, Tyler's childhood wasn't without its difficulties. He attended 12 different schools across the Los Angeles and Sacramento areas, a result of his family's frequent moves and financial instability. This constant change forced him to adapt quickly, shaping his resilient and outgoing personality. Despite the instability, Tyler found ways to channel his energy into creative pursuits, often finding solace in music and art.

As he grew older, the melting pot of cultures in Los Angeles began to inform Tyler's artistic vision. The city's diversity allowed him to explore various subcultures, from skateboarding and punk rock to hip-hop and fashion. This eclectic mix of influences became the cornerstone of his artistic identity, enabling him to break boundaries and redefine what it meant to be a rapper and a creator.

Tyler's journey wasn't limited to music during his formative years. Before rising to fame, he worked at Starbucks for over two years and briefly at FedEx. These jobs not only provided him with financial support but also gave him a glimpse into the working world, further fueling his determination to succeed on his own terms.

Tyler's upbringing in Los Angeles, combined with his mother's unwavering support and exposure to diverse cultural influences, laid the foundation for his success. The challenges he faced, from an absent father to financial instability, became fuel for his creativity and ambition. These formative years not only shaped his unique sound but also instilled in him the determination to carve his own path in the music industry. Tyler's early life is a testament to the power of resilience, creativity, and the pursuit of one's passions.

Chapter 2: The Rise of Odd Future

Formation of Odd Future

Odd Future, short for Odd Future Wolf Gang Kill Them All (OFWGKTA), was formed in 2007 by Tyler, The Creator and a group of like-minded friends who shared a passion for music, skateboarding, and visual art. The collective included Earl Sweatshirt, Casey Veggies, Frank Ocean, Hodgy Beats, Left Brain, Syd tha Kyd, Domo Genesis, Jasper Dolphin, and Taco Bennett, among others. The group initially came together in Los Angeles as a tight-knit community of misfits who bonded over their unconventional interests and mutual desire to create without boundaries.

Tyler emerged as the group's de facto leader, using his vision and work ethic to guide the collective's artistic direction. Odd Future was not just a rap group—it was a multidisciplinary movement that included music, graphic design, and comedy. From the outset, Tyler emphasized complete creative freedom, encouraging the members to push the limits of expression and challenge mainstream norms.

Odd Future began releasing music independently on Tumblr, leveraging the platform to reach their audience directly. This DIY approach not only resonated with their fanbase but also became a hallmark of their ethos. The group's early material was raw, energetic, and unapologetically rebellious, reflecting their disdain for traditional industry expectations.

Breakout Mixtape "Bastard" and Its Impact

In 2009, Tyler released his debut studio album, "Bastard", which became a turning point for Odd Future. The project, produced almost entirely by

Tyler himself, introduced his dark, introspective, and often controversial style to the world. Bastard revolves around the fictional narrative of Tyler in a therapy session with his imaginary therapist, Dr. TC. The mixtape delved into themes of abandonment, self-doubt, and frustration, giving listeners a raw glimpse into Tyler's psyche.

Track like "French!" showcased Tyler's talent for blending gritty, haunting production with sharp, provocative lyrics. "Bastard" resonated with a young audience that felt alienated by mainstream culture, offering an unfiltered voice for their discontent. The album's edgy aesthetic and unconventional approach earned widespread attention, catapulting Tyler and Odd Future into the spotlight.

Although "Bastard" faced criticism for its controversial lyrics, it also garnered praise for its originality and fearlessness. The album's success proved that Odd Future was more than just a group of rebellious teenagers—they were a legitimate creative force capable of redefining hip-hop.

Odd Future's Cultural Movement

With the release of "Bastard", Odd Future's influence began to spread beyond music. The collective's irreverent style, DIY mentality, and boundary-pushing creativity sparked a cultural movement that resonated with a generation of young fans. Odd Future wasn't just a group—it was a lifestyle. From their chaotic live performances to their distinctive fashion sense, the group cultivated an image that was equal parts punk rock and hip-hop, blending genres and aesthetics in ways that had rarely been seen before.

Odd Future's rise coincided with the advent of social media, which they used to amplify their reach. Platforms like Tumblr, Twitter, and YouTube became essential tools for the group to share their music, videos, and personalities with fans. Tyler's use of social media, in particular, showcased his wit and irreverence, helping to build a devoted online following.

In 2012, the group released the compilation album "The OF Tape Vol. 2", which further cemented their place in hip-hop. Tracks like "Oldie" highlighted the collective's diversity, with each member bringing their unique style to the table. The album's success led to a sold-out tour, where the group's high-energy performances and antics gained legendary status.

Odd Future also expanded their brand into other ventures, including the sketch comedy show "Loiter Squad" on Adult Swim and the launch of their own clothing line, Odd Future Clothing. These projects reflected their multidimensional approach to creativity, demonstrating that they were not confined to any single medium.

By challenging societal norms and embracing individuality, Odd Future inspired countless fans to embrace their own authenticity. The group's impact extended beyond music, influencing fashion, art, and even social attitudes toward creativity and self-expression.

Odd Future eventually disbanded in the mid-2010s as its members pursued solo careers, but their legacy as a cultural movement endures. Tyler, The Creator's leadership and artistic vision were instrumental in the group's success, setting the stage for his evolution as one of the most innovative and influential artists of his generation. Through Odd Future, Tyler and his collaborators redefined what it meant to be an artist in the 21st century, proving that creativity knows no boundaries.

Chapter 3: Breakthrough with Goblin

The Success of "Yonkers"

Tyler, The Creator's breakthrough moment came with the release of his second studio album, "Goblin", in May 2011. At the forefront of the album's success was its lead single, "Yonkers." The track, released earlier that year, became an unexpected cultural phenomenon. Accompanied by a self-directed music video, "Yonkers" showcased Tyler's raw talent as a rapper, producer, and visual artist.

The video, which featured Tyler sitting in a dark, minimalist setting while rapping to the camera, was both unsettling and captivating. Its most memorable moment involved Tyler holding a cockroach, letting it crawl on him, and then appearing to eat it. This shocking imagery, combined with his gritty lyrics and monotone delivery, sparked widespread attention. The video quickly went viral, earning millions of views on YouTube and catapulting Tyler into the public eye.

"Yonkers" was praised for its haunting production, featuring a stripped-down beat layered with ominous bass and eerie melodies. The song's lyrics, filled with introspection, frustration, and moments of dark humor, reflected Tyler's struggle to navigate his newfound fame and the expectations placed upon him. While controversial, the track resonated with a generation that connected with its themes of rebellion and alienation.

The success of "Yonkers" not only cemented Tyler as a rising star but also put Odd Future on the map as a collective to watch. The song earned Tyler the MTV Video Music Award for Best New Artist in 2011.

Public Reception and Controversy

The release of "Goblin" was met with a mix of acclaim and criticism. Fans and critics alike praised Tyler's bold approach to storytelling, his unfiltered lyricism, and his ability to create a dark, immersive atmosphere. Tracks like "Radicals," "She," and "Sandwitches" highlighted his versatility as an artist, blending provocative themes with moments of vulnerability and humor.

However, Goblin was not without its controversies. Tyler's lyrics often delved into themes of violence, misogyny, and taboo subjects, sparking backlash from critics and activists. Some accused him of promoting harmful messages, while others defended his work as a form of artistic expression. Tyler responded to the criticism by emphasizing the fictional nature of his lyrics, comparing his storytelling to that of filmmakers or novelists who explore dark themes.

Despite the polarizing reception, Goblin was a commercial success. The album debuted at No. 5 on the Billboard 200 chart, selling over 45,000 copies in its first week. Its success was a testament to Tyler's ability to connect with an audience that valued authenticity and unconventional artistry.

Tyler's public persona during this time further fueled his rise to fame. Known for his outspoken nature and irreverent humor, he often clashed with critics and media outlets while maintaining a devoted fanbase. His interviews and social media presence showcased his wit and unfiltered personality, making him a compelling figure in hip-hop and pop culture.

Establishing His Identity in Hip-Hop

With the release of Goblin, Tyler, The Creator firmly established himself as a unique voice in hip-hop. He rejected the conventions of the genre, blending elements of horrorcore, jazz, and experimental production to create a sound that was entirely his own. His self-produced tracks demonstrated his skill as a musician, with intricate beats and layered compositions that challenged traditional hip-hop norms.

Goblin also marked the beginning of Tyler's exploration of his identity as an artist. The album's central narrative followed the character of Dr. TC, a fictional therapist guiding Tyler through his thoughts and emotions. This introspective framework allowed Tyler to confront his insecurities, ambitions, and frustrations, creating a deeply personal and relatable body of work.

As Tyler's profile grew, so did his influence on the broader cultural landscape. He became a symbol of individuality and creative freedom, inspiring a generation of artists and fans to embrace their authentic selves. His ability to defy categorization and push the boundaries of hip-hop earned him respect from peers and critics alike, solidifying his place as a trailblazer in the industry.

In hindsight, "Goblin" was more than just an album—it was a statement. It announced Tyler, The Creator as an artist unafraid to take risks, challenge norms, and provoke thought. While it may not have been free from flaws or controversy, its impact on hip-hop and pop culture was undeniable. Goblin laid the foundation for Tyler's continued evolution as an artist, paving the way for the groundbreaking work that would follow. Through its success and the cultural waves it created, Goblin marked the moment when Tyler went from an underground sensation to a bona fide force in music.

Chapter 4: Musical Evolution and Experimentation

Albums: "Wolf", "Cherry Bomb", "Flower Boy", "Igor", and "Call Me If You Get Lost"

Tyler, The Creator's career has been defined by his constant musical reinvention. Each of his albums represents a distinct phase in his artistic journey, showcasing his evolving sound and creative ambition.

Following the success of Goblin, Tyler released "Wolf" in 2013, a deeply personal album that explored themes of love, abandonment, and self-discovery. While maintaining his dark, confrontational style, Wolf introduced more sophisticated production techniques and a broader emotional range. Songs like "Awkward" and "Answer" offered glimpses of vulnerability, while tracks like "IFHY" displayed his knack for blending introspection with bold experimentation.

In 2015, "Cherry Bomb" marked a significant departure from Tyler's earlier work. The album leaned heavily into distorted, chaotic production, drawing influences from punk, jazz, and R&B. Critics were divided on the album's abrasive sound, but it demonstrated Tyler's willingness to take risks and push boundaries. Tracks like "Find Your Wings" and "Smuckers" highlighted his growth as a producer, incorporating lush instrumentation and dynamic arrangements.

Tyler's 2017 album "Flower Boy" represented a watershed moment in his career. The album was a vibrant, introspective exploration of identity, love, and loneliness, earning widespread critical acclaim. Songs like "See You Again" and "Boredom" showcased Tyler's melodic sensibilities, while tracks like "Garden Shed" subtly addressed his journey with self-acceptance and sexuality. Flower Boy was a commercial success and marked Tyler's first Grammy solo nomination, signaling his transition from a provocative outsider to a respected artist.

In 2019, Tyler released "Igor", an innovative album that blended hip-hop, R&B, and soul to explore the complexities of a turbulent romantic relationship. Through the persona of Igor, Tyler conveyed raw emotion in tracks like "EARFQUAKE" and "A BOY IS A GUN." The album received widespread critical acclaim, debuting at number one on the US Billboard 200—Tyler's first chart-topping album in the United States. This success earned him his first Grammy Award for Best Rap Album, further establishing his reputation as a visionary artist capable of crafting deeply emotional and genre-defying projects.

Tyler's album, "Call Me If You Get Lost" (2021), marked a return to his rap roots while maintaining his penchant for experimentation. The album featured a travel-themed narrative, with Tyler assuming the persona of "Sir Baudelaire," a sophisticated globetrotter. Songs like "LUMBERJACK" and "HOT WIND BLOWS" blended braggadocio with introspection, while tracks like "WUSYANAME" and "SWEET/I THOUGHT YOU WANTED TO DANCE" showcased his melodic growth. The album earned Tyler his second Grammy for Best Rap Album, further solidifying his legacy.

Transition from Rap to Melodic and Experimental Styles

One of Tyler's most defining traits as an artist is his willingness to evolve. Early in his career, he was known for his raw, aggressive rap style and dark, confrontational lyrics. However, as he matured, Tyler began incorporating more melodic elements into his music, drawing inspiration from genres like soul, funk, and jazz.

This transition was evident on Wolf, where tracks like "Treehome95" featured lush, jazzy instrumentation, and became more pronounced on Cherry Bomb, with its experimental soundscapes. By the time "Flower Boy" arrived, Tyler had fully embraced a melodic, introspective style, crafting songs that were as emotionally resonant as they were sonically innovative.

With Igor, Tyler took his experimentation to new heights, creating an album that defied traditional genre classifications. The project relied heavily on vocal modulation, layered harmonies, and unconventional song structures, showcasing Tyler's growth as a producer and songwriter. While "Call Me If You Get Lost" saw him return to his rap roots, it also highlighted his ability to seamlessly integrate diverse influences, from brash hip-hop to elegant R&B.

Themes and Narratives in His Music

Throughout his career, Tyler's music has been characterized by its rich themes and compelling narratives. Early in his career, his work often dealt with themes of rebellion, angst, and alienation, resonating with fans who felt similarly misunderstood. As he matured, his music began to explore deeper emotional territory, tackling issues like identity, love, and self-acceptance.

In "Wolf," Tyler explored his difficult relationship with his absent father, while "Flower Boy" touched on feelings of loneliness, unrequited love, and self-exploration. Many viewed the album as a declaration of his sexuality, with songs like "Garden Shed" and "I Ain't Got Time!" offering subtle hints about his journey.

"Igor" took listeners through the ups and downs of a romantic relationship, with Tyler using the persona of Igor to examine themes of heartbreak, jealousy, and self-esteem. The album's narrative progression, from the joyful "EARFQUAKE" to the poignant "ARE WE STILL FRIENDS?", highlighted Tyler's talent for creating emotionally impactful stories.

With "Call Me If You Get Lost", Tyler embraced themes of adventure, self-confidence, and growth, presenting himself as a more mature, self-assured artist. The album's travel-themed narrative served as a metaphor for his personal and artistic journey, reflecting his evolution over the years.

Through his musical evolution and experimentation, Tyler, The Creator has proven himself to be one of the most innovative and influential artists of his generation. His ability to push boundaries while staying true to his artistic vision has cemented his place as a pioneer in modern music.

Chapter 5: Creative Ventures Beyond Music

Golf Wang Clothing Line and Merchandising

In 2011, Tyler, The Creator launched his own clothing line, Golf Wang, a bold and vibrant extension of his personality and artistic vision. The brand's name is a playful twist on "Wolf Gang," a reference to Odd Future's catchphrase. Golf Wang became known for its daring use of bright colors, quirky patterns, and provocative designs that stood in stark contrast to the muted tones and minimalism dominating streetwear at the time.

Tyler has consistently infused his unique sense of humor and creativity into Golf Wang, making it an extension of his artistry. From graphic tees featuring irreverent slogans to colorful sneakers and outerwear, the brand has cultivated a loyal following among fans and fashion enthusiasts alike. Golf Wang's seasonal collections are often accompanied by lookbooks and videos directed by Tyler, showcasing his ability to create cohesive visual narratives.

The brand has also expanded into collaborations with major companies, such as Converse. Tyler's partnership with Converse led to the release of the Golf Le Fleur sneaker line, featuring playful, pastel-colored takes on Converse's classic designs. These collaborations further cemented Tyler's influence in the fashion world, bridging the gap between streetwear and high-end design.

Beyond clothing, Tyler has turned Golf Wang into a cultural phenomenon with events like the annual Camp Flog Gnaw Carnival. The festival, named after Odd Future's phrase spelled backward, combines music, fashion, and entertainment, offering fans a glimpse into Tyler's eclectic world. Through Golf Wang, Tyler has established himself not only as a musician but as a visionary entrepreneur.

TV Show "Loiter Squad" and Acting Roles

In 2012, Tyler ventured into television with Loiter Squad, a sketch comedy series created by Odd Future and produced by Dickhouse Productions, the team behind "Jackass". The show aired on Adult Swim and featured Tyler alongside other Odd Future members like Earl Sweatshirt and Jasper Dolphin. Loiter Squad blended absurd humor, pranks, and surreal sketches, showcasing the group's comedic talents and offbeat sensibilities.

The show ran for three seasons and became a cult favorite among fans of Odd Future's irreverent style. Tyler's comedic timing and charisma were evident in his standout performances, from playing outrageous characters to participating in over-the-top stunts. While Loiter Squad was primarily a comedic endeavor, it demonstrated Tyler's versatility and willingness to explore new creative avenues outside of music.

In addition to Loiter Squad, Tyler has made cameo appearances in other projects, further showcasing his acting abilities. His unique personality and humor have translated well to the screen, earning him opportunities in animated series like "The Jellies!", which he co-created. The show, which aired on Adult Swim, follows the adventures of a jellyfish family and features Tyler voicing one of the main characters. His foray into animation highlighted his interest in storytelling and visual creativity.

Directing Music Videos and Visual Artistry

Tyler, The Creator has long been recognized for his distinctive visual style, which extends to his work as a music video director. Using the pseudonym Wolf

Haley, Tyler has directed most of his own music videos, as well as videos for other artists. His direction often blends vivid imagery, bold concepts, and a touch of absurdity, making his videos instantly recognizable.

Early in his career, Tyler's videos, such as "Yonkers," captured attention for their raw, minimalist approach and provocative imagery. The black-and-white video for "Yonkers," featuring Tyler eating a cockroach and staring intensely into the camera, became a viral sensation and set the tone for his unique aesthetic.

As his music evolved, so did his visual artistry. Videos for songs like "See You Again" and "EARFQUAKE" showcased a more polished and cinematic style, with intricate set designs and storytelling elements. Tyler's attention to detail and hands-on approach ensure that his videos are a true reflection of his artistic vision.

Beyond music videos, Tyler has expanded his visual artistry to include album covers, merchandise designs, and short films. His creative direction for albums like "Igor" and "Call Me If You Get Lost" extended beyond the music, creating cohesive visual identities that enhanced the listening experience. From the pastel-hued aesthetic of "Igor" to the travel-themed visuals of "Call Me If You Get Lost", Tyler's ability to craft immersive worlds has set him apart as a multidisciplinary artist.

Through ventures like Golf Wang, Loiter Squad, and his visual projects, Tyler, The Creator has demonstrated a remarkable ability to excel across multiple creative domains. His entrepreneurial spirit, comedic talent, and visual artistry have made him a cultural icon, proving that his creativity knows no bounds. These endeavors not only complement his music but also highlight his evolution into a multifaceted artist and innovator.

Chapter 6: Awards and Recognition

Grammy Wins and Nominations

Tyler, The Creator's career has been marked by multiple Grammy wins and nominations, underscoring his status as one of the most innovative and boundary-pushing artists in modern music. His journey with the Grammys began in 2013 when he earned his first nomination for Album of the Year as a featured artist on Frank Ocean's "Channel Orange". This nomination was a testament to his early influence on shaping the sound of contemporary hip-hop and R&B.

In 2017, Tyler's fourth studio album, Flower Boy, received a nomination forbBest Rap Album at the 60th Annual Grammy Awards. Though it didn't win, the nomination reflected his evolution as a rapper, producer, and songwriter, as the album featured introspective themes and genre-defying production.

Tyler's first Grammy win came in 2020 with his fifth studio album, IGOR. The critically acclaimed project, blending rap with soul, funk, and electronic elements, won the award for Best Rap Album at the 62nd Annual Grammy Awards. This victory was particularly significant as Tyler expressed during his acceptance speech that IGOR didn't fit the traditional mold of a rap album, highlighting the broader conversation about genre classifications in awards.

In 2022, Tyler repeated this achievement with his sixth album, "Call Me If You Get Lost", which won Best Rap Album at the 64th Annual Grammy Awards. This marked his second Grammy win in the same category, further solidifying his consistency in delivering high-quality, boundary-breaking work. Additionally, the album's single "WusYaName," featuring YoungBoy Never

Broke Again and Ty Dolla $ign, was nominated for Best Melodic Rap Performance, showcasing Tyler's ability to create versatile and innovative music.

Cultural Impact and Influence on Modern Artists

Beyond awards, Tyler, The Creator's influence on modern artists and culture is profound. As the founder and leader of Odd Future, a collective that included Frank Ocean, Earl Sweatshirt, Syd, and others, Tyler spearheaded a movement that redefined the sound and aesthetic of hip-hop in the 2010s. Odd Future's unapologetically rebellious spirit, DIY ethos, and experimental approach to music inspired countless artists to embrace their individuality and take creative risks.

Tyler's success has also broken barriers for unconventional artists in hip-hop. His genre-defying music, blending rap with elements of jazz, funk, and R&B, paved the way for artists like

Billie Eilish, and BROCKHAMPTON. He challenged the industry's norms with his bold self-expression, often addressing themes of identity, sexuality, and mental health in his music. This vulnerability resonated with fans and helped expand the definition of what hip-hop could be.

Tyler's influence extends to fashion, where his Golf Wang clothing line and distinct personal style have left a lasting imprint. His ability to seamlessly merge music, fashion, and visual art has created a multi-dimensional brand that continues to inspire young creators worldwide.

Legacy as a Boundary-Breaking Artist

Tyler, The Creator's legacy is defined by his fearless approach to art and his refusal to conform to industry standards. His early work, characterized by raw, often controversial lyrics and minimalist production, laid the foundation for a career built on reinvention. With each album, Tyler pushed the boundaries of genre and self-expression, evolving from the rebellious teenager of Goblin to the refined and introspective artist behind IGOR and Call Me If You Get Lost.

As a director and visual artist, Tyler's music videos, often created under the pseudonym Wolf Haley, have further established his reputation as a visionary. His innovative visuals, such as the unsettling "Yonkers" video or the vibrant and surreal aesthetic of "IGOR", have redefined how artists can use visual storytelling to complement their music.

Moreover, Tyler's ability to navigate controversy and use it as a platform for growth has shaped his public persona. From being banned in countries like the UK due to his provocative lyrics to winning awards in the same regions, his journey reflects resilience and the power of staying true to one's artistry.

Tyler's impact is also evident in the recognition he's received beyond music. He has won a Brit Award for International Male Solo Artist, multiple BET Hip Hop Awards, and several UK Music Video Awards. These accolades highlight his influence across different cultural landscapes and his ability to connect with audiences globally.

Chapter 7: Personal Life and Philosophy

Views on Identity and Sexuality

Tyler, The Creator has consistently addressed issues of identity and sexuality in his work. Since the outset of his career, his lyrics and interviews have generated discussions about his private life, even as he intentionally leaves many details unclear. His music often alludes to same-sex relationships, notably in his 2017 album Flower Boy, where he raps, "I've been kissing white boys since 2004" in the track "I Ain't Got Time!" This line was largely seen as an indication of Tyler coming out, although he has never clearly defined his sexual orientation.

In interviews, Tyler has approached the subject with humor and deflection, suggesting that he values the freedom to express himself without being confined to societal expectations or labels. His approach to identity reflects a broader philosophy of fluidity and self-acceptance. He embraces the idea that people should feel empowered to explore their identities without the need for explanation or validation from others. This perspective resonates with his fans, many of whom find solace in his unapologetic self-expression.

Perspectives on Fame and Individuality

Tyler's views on fame are similarly nuanced. While he has achieved immense success, he has always emphasized the importance of staying true to himself. He has often criticized the pressures and superficialities of fame, opting instead to focus on creating art that reflects his personal growth and interests. In interviews, Tyler has expressed frustration with being boxed into categories, whether as a rapper, a celebrity, or a public figure.

This resistance to conformity is a recurring theme in Tyler's work and life. He has built his career on defying expectations, from his early days with Odd Future to his evolution as a genre-defying artist. Tyler frequently speaks about the value of individuality, encouraging others to embrace their unique qualities and passions. This philosophy is evident in his ventures outside of music, such as his Golf Wang clothing line, which showcases his distinctive aesthetic and creative vision.

Tyler's individuality also extends to his approach to success. He has often remarked that he prioritizes creative fulfillment over commercial validation. His albums, such as IGOR and Call Me If You Get Lost, are testament to his willingness to take risks and push boundaries, even if it means alienating certain audiences. For Tyler, success is not measured by chart positions or awards but by his ability to create art that feels authentic and innovative.

Relationships and Friendships in the Industry

Despite his rebellious persona, Tyler has forged meaningful relationships within the music industry. His close-knit circle includes collaborators from Odd Future, such as Frank Ocean, Earl Sweatshirt, and Syd. These relationships were instrumental in his early career, providing a supportive environment for experimentation and growth. While Odd Future has since disbanded, Tyler has maintained strong connections with many of its members, often citing their influence on his artistic development.

Tyler's friendship with A$AP Rocky is another notable example of his industry relationships. The two artists have frequently collaborated and publicly supported each other, showcasing a genuine camaraderie that contrasts with the competitive nature of the music world. Their bond highlights Tyler's appreciation for creative partnerships and his ability to connect with like-minded individuals.

In addition to his industry friendships, Tyler values relationships that inspire and challenge him. He has often spoken about his admiration for artists who prioritize authenticity and innovation, such as Pharrell Williams, Kanye West, and Erykah Badu. These influences have shaped his approach to music and life, reinforcing his belief in the importance of staying true to one's vision.

However, Tyler has also been candid about the challenges of maintaining relationships in the spotlight. The demands of fame and the pressure to constantly produce can strain personal connections, a reality he has addressed in songs like "Answer" and "November." Despite these challenges, Tyler remains committed to cultivating relationships that enrich his life and creativity.

Chapter 8: Tyler's Influence on Culture and Fashion

Role in Redefining Masculinity in Hip-Hop

Tyler, The Creator has played a key role in redefining traditional ideas of masculinity in hip-hop. Renowned for his daring and unorthodox persona, he has continually pushed back against the hyper-masculine clichés commonly linked to rap. Whether during his time with Odd Future or in his latest albums, Tyler has embraced vulnerability, emotional openness, and creativity, expanding the definition of masculinity within the genre.

In songs like "See You Again" and "EARFQUAKE," Tyler explores themes of love, heartbreak, and self-doubt, topics that were once considered atypical for the genre. His willingness to share these emotions has inspired a new generation of artists to prioritize authenticity over bravado. Tyler's nonconformity extends to his public persona as well, where his playful humor, eccentric mannerisms, and refusal to fit into traditional molds have earned him both acclaim and criticism.

Tyler has also challenged gender norms through his style. He frequently experiments with colorful and androgynous clothing, wearing pastel suits, floral prints, and accessories traditionally associated with femininity. By doing so, he has opened up a dialogue about self-expression, proving that masculinity can coexist with flamboyance and softness. This redefinition of masculinity has resonated deeply with fans, particularly younger audiences who see Tyler as a symbol of liberation and self-acceptance.

Contributions to Fashion and Style

Tyler's impact on fashion is as significant as his contributions to music. In 2011, he founded Golf Wang, a clothing line that reflects his vibrant and eclectic aesthetic. The brand is known for its bold colors, unique patterns, and irreverent designs, often featuring playful graphics, slogans, and themes that mirror Tyler's personality. Unlike many celebrity fashion lines, Golf Wang stands out for its originality, avoiding trends in favor of creating a distinct visual identity.

Tyler's style has evolved over the years, from the skate-inspired looks of his Odd Future days to the refined, vintage-inspired ensembles he favors today. His fashion choices often blend elements of preppy, retro, and streetwear styles, creating a look that is both nostalgic and forward-thinking. This evolution is evident in his music videos, performances, and public appearances, where his outfits often make as much of a statement as his art.

Beyond Golf Wang, Tyler launched a footwear collaboration with Converse in 2017, introducing the Golf Le Fleur line. This partnership produced a range of sneakers featuring vibrant colors and floral motifs, which quickly became highly sought after by fans and sneaker enthusiasts. The success of Golf Le Fleur solidified Tyler's status as a fashion innovator, further blurring the lines between music and style.

Endorsements and Collaborations

Tyler's influence in the fashion world has led to numerous endorsements and collaborations with major brands. In addition to his work with Converse, he has partnered with companies like Lacoste and Levi's, creating capsule collections that showcase his distinct creative vision. These collaborations often emphasize quality, craftsmanship, and originality, aligning with Tyler's emphasis on authenticity.

One of his most notable collaborations is his work with Lacoste, where he reimagined the brand's iconic polo shirts and accessories with bold colors and modern silhouettes. The collection received widespread praise for its playful yet sophisticated approach, reflecting Tyler's ability to merge high fashion with streetwear sensibilities.

Tyler's endorsements extend beyond fashion, as he has appeared in campaigns for brands like Coca-Cola and Mountain Dew. While his approach to partnerships is selective, he ensures that each collaboration aligns with his personal brand and values. This careful curation has allowed Tyler to maintain his credibility while expanding his influence across industries.

Cultural Influence Beyond Fashion

Tyler's impact on culture extends far beyond the realms of music and fashion. As an artist, he has created a multi-dimensional brand that encompasses music, clothing, visual art, and film.

His ability to seamlessly integrate these mediums has inspired a new generation of creatives to explore interdisciplinary approaches to their work.

Through his boldness and individuality, Tyler has become a role model for self-expression and artistic freedom. His cultural influence is particularly evident in the ways younger artists and fans emulate his style, adopt his fearless attitude, and embrace his ethos of authenticity. From challenging traditional masculinity to redefining the boundaries of hip-hop, Tyler has carved out a unique space for himself in contemporary culture, leaving an indelible mark on both the music and fashion industries.

Chapter 9: Controversies and Public Image

Lyrics, Bans, and Public Reactions

From the beginning of his career, Tyler, The Creator has been a lightning rod for controversy. His provocative lyrics and irreverent persona in the early days of Odd Future often drew sharp criticism. Songs from his debut mixtape "Bastard" and subsequent album "Goblin" included graphic and violent imagery, as well as themes that critics deemed offensive, including homophobia and misogyny. Tyler defended his work as a form of storytelling and artistic expression, emphasizing that his lyrics were fictional and reflective of his dark humor rather than his personal beliefs.

The backlash, however, extended beyond criticism. In 2015, Tyler was banned from entering the United Kingdom due to the content of his earlier lyrics, which authorities claimed encouraged violence and hatred. This decision sparked widespread debate about censorship and freedom of expression, with many artists and fans rallying in his defense. Similarly, Tyler faced a ban in New Zealand in 2014, which was later lifted. These incidents not only amplified his notoriety but also underscored the tension between his creative vision and societal norms.

Public reactions to Tyler's controversies have been polarizing. While some viewed him as a provocateur pushing the boundaries of art, others labeled him a harmful influence. Over time, however, Tyler's artistry began to overshadow the controversies, as he demonstrated growth both personally and musically. His ability to channel his rebellious energy into more mature and nuanced projects allowed him to reframe his public image.

Growth and Evolution Over the Years

Despite his tumultuous start, Tyler has shown remarkable growth throughout his career. His evolution is most evident in his music, where he transitioned from abrasive, shock-value-driven content to introspective, emotionally rich storytelling. Albums like Flower Boy (2017) marked a turning point, showcasing a more vulnerable side of Tyler as he explored themes of love, identity, and self-acceptance. Critics and fans alike praised the album for its depth, earning Tyler his first Grammy nomination for Best Rap Album.

This transformation extended to his public persona. In interviews and public appearances, Tyler began to distance himself from the confrontational image of his early career. His humor remained sharp, but he became more thoughtful and reflective, openly discussing topics like his sexuality, creative process, and aspirations. Tyler's candidness resonated with fans, many of whom admired his willingness to address past mistakes and embrace growth.

One of the most significant aspects of Tyler's evolution has been his shift toward inclusivity. While his earlier work faced accusations of homophobia, he later used his platform to celebrate individuality and challenge stereotypes. Tyler himself hinted at his own queerness in songs like "Garden Shed" from Flower Boy and "I THINK" from IGOR (2019). These revelations, though subtle, helped him connect with a broader audience and positioned him as an advocate for authenticity and self-expression.

Tyler's visual and creative projects have also contributed to his changing image. His music videos, often self-directed, showcase a sophisticated artistic vision that blends humor, surrealism, and cinematic storytelling. Similarly, his ventures in fashion and television, such as the Golf Wang clothing line and the comedy series Loiter Squad, highlight his versatility and entrepreneurial spirit.

Reframing His Public Image

Today, Tyler, The Creator is celebrated not just as a rapper, but as a multi-dimensional artist who has successfully redefined his narrative. While his early controversies remain a part of his story, they are now viewed as stepping stones in his journey toward self-awareness and maturity. His ability to confront criticism, learn from it, and use it as fuel for growth has earned him widespread respect, even among former detractors.

Tyler's transformation is also a testament to the evolving cultural landscape. The same industry and audiences that once shunned him have embraced his boundary-pushing creativity and unapologetic individuality. In many ways, Tyler embodies the modern artist: one who is unafraid to take risks, acknowledge flaws, and continuously reinvent themselves.

Chapter 10: The Future of Tyler, the Creator

Potential Ventures in Film, Fashion, and Business

Tyler's ambitions extend far beyond music. His creative ventures in film, fashion, and business suggest a future filled with diverse opportunities. Having directed many of his music videos, Tyler has demonstrated a keen eye for visual storytelling. His aesthetic—marked by surrealism, bold colors, and innovative camera work—has the potential to translate into filmmaking. Whether as a director, actor, or writer, Tyler's involvement in the film industry could bring a fresh perspective to modern cinema.

In fashion, Tyler's Golf Wang brand continues to thrive as a hub for bold and unconventional designs. The brand's emphasis on vibrant colors and playful patterns has earned it a dedicated following, and its collaborations with major companies like Converse have cemented its cultural relevance. Looking ahead, Tyler might expand Golf Wang into new areas, such as luxury apparel or sustainable fashion. Given his entrepreneurial spirit, he could also launch entirely new brands or collaborate with iconic fashion houses to create exclusive collections.

Tyler has also shown interest in broader business ventures, often speaking about the importance of ownership and creative freedom. His future may include investments in technology, media platforms, or even education initiatives aimed at empowering young creators. By leveraging his influence and resources, Tyler has the potential to become a significant figure in industries outside of music and fashion.

His Lasting Impact on Art and Music

As Tyler, the Creator continues to evolve, his legacy as an artist is already firmly established. He has redefined what it means to be a hip-hop artist, blending genres like R&B, pop, and jazz to create a sound that is uniquely his own. Albums such as IGOR and Flower Boy have influenced a new wave of artists who are unafraid to explore vulnerability and experiment with their music.

Tyler's impact extends beyond his music. He has helped shift cultural conversations around masculinity, queerness, and individuality in hip-hop, encouraging others to embrace their authentic selves. His unapologetic approach to self-expression has inspired countless fans and artists, proving that success does not require conformity.

Moreover, Tyler's commitment to creating holistic artistic experiences—complete with cohesive visuals, narratives, and performances—has raised the bar for modern musicians. By treating his albums as comprehensive works of art, he has set a standard for storytelling and creativity that resonates across generations.

Conclusion

Tyler, the Creator's legacy is no simple task, as his influence spans music, fashion, culture, and beyond. From his early days as the audacious leader of Odd Future to becoming a Grammy-winning artist and creative visionary, Tyler's journey embodies the power of authenticity, innovation, and resilience. He has shattered stereotypes within hip-hop, championed individuality, and created a space where vulnerability and experimentation are celebrated.

At the heart of Tyler's legacy lies his refusal to conform. His music, marked by its genre-defying nature and deeply personal narratives, has consistently challenged industry norms. Albums like "IGOR" and "Call Me If You Get Lost" showcase his ability to evolve as an artist, blending his signature boldness with introspection and storytelling. Tyler's impact on the music world is undeniable, as he has inspired a generation of artists to embrace their uniqueness and push creative boundaries.

Beyond music, Tyler has left an indelible mark on fashion and visual artistry. His Golf Wang brand has become a symbol of individuality, and his vibrant aesthetic has redefined contemporary style. His work in directing music videos and creating cohesive visual narratives underscores his commitment to delivering art that is immersive and multifaceted. Tyler's ventures remind us that creativity knows no bounds when paired with passion and determination.

Perhaps most notably, Tyler's journey serves as a beacon for those who feel out of place in a world that often demands conformity. He has shown that success can be achieved on one's own terms, and that vulnerability and self-expression are not weaknesses but strengths. His openness about identity, struggles, and aspirations has resonated deeply with fans, creating a connection that transcends traditional boundaries between artist and audience.

As Tyler, the Creator continues to innovate and inspire, his legacy is far from complete. He remains a dynamic force in the cultural landscape, constantly redefining what it means to be an artist. His influence will undoubtedly endure, not only in the art he creates but in the lives he has touched and the barriers he has broken.

In the end, Tyler's story is a testament to the transformative power of creativity and self-belief. It is a reminder that true artistry lies not in following trends, but in setting them. Tyler, the Creator's legacy is one of fearless exploration, profound impact, and unwavering authenticity—a legacy that will inspire generations to come.

Printed in Dunstable, United Kingdom